Copyright Message:

© 2025 ALINA STETSYUK

All rights reserved. No part of this publication may be reproduced, distributed, or transmitted in any form or by any means, including photocopying, recording, or other electronic or mechanical methods, without the prior written permission of the publisher, except in the case of brief quotations embodied in critical reviews and certain other noncommercial uses permitted by copyright law. For permissions requests or inquiries, contact alinastetsyukwriter@gmail.com

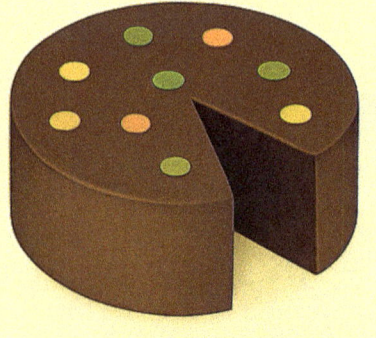

Dear Readers,

Welcome to Everything Equal—a heartwarming story about fairness, feelings, and growing up. Peter believes everyone should get an equal slice of life (and cake!), but he soon learns that real fairness is more than simple rules.

This gentle tale helps children explore the balance between justice and kindness, showing that empathy often matters more than being exact.

We hope it brings smiles, sparks reflection, and starts meaningful conversations.

        Warm regards,
        Alina Stetsyuk

Miguel liked it when everything was equal. Apples from the garden? Split with friends. Candy from guests? Share with his brother. Bakugans at school? Everyone gets the same.

Miguel believed in one rule: Everything is equal—so no one feels left out.

But the world isn't black and white.
It's colorful and full of surprises.
Sometimes, things just can't be divided like in math class.

One sunny Sunday morning, Miguel and his little brother woke up early. They brushed their teeth, did exercises, and even cleaned their room—just like Mom and Dad taught them!

Then, they remembered the cake! Grandma had baked it with love for Miguel's birthday. There were a few slices left. Yum!

The boys licked their lips.
The little brother snuck a bite!
"Hey!" Miguel cried.
"Now, someone might not get a piece!"

Miguel cut the cake into four slices.

"Grab the plates," he told his brother.

"For Grandma?" the little one joked.

"No! For us—oh wait. Grandma and Grandpa didn't get any yesterday!"

Only four slices.
Six people.
Uh-oh.

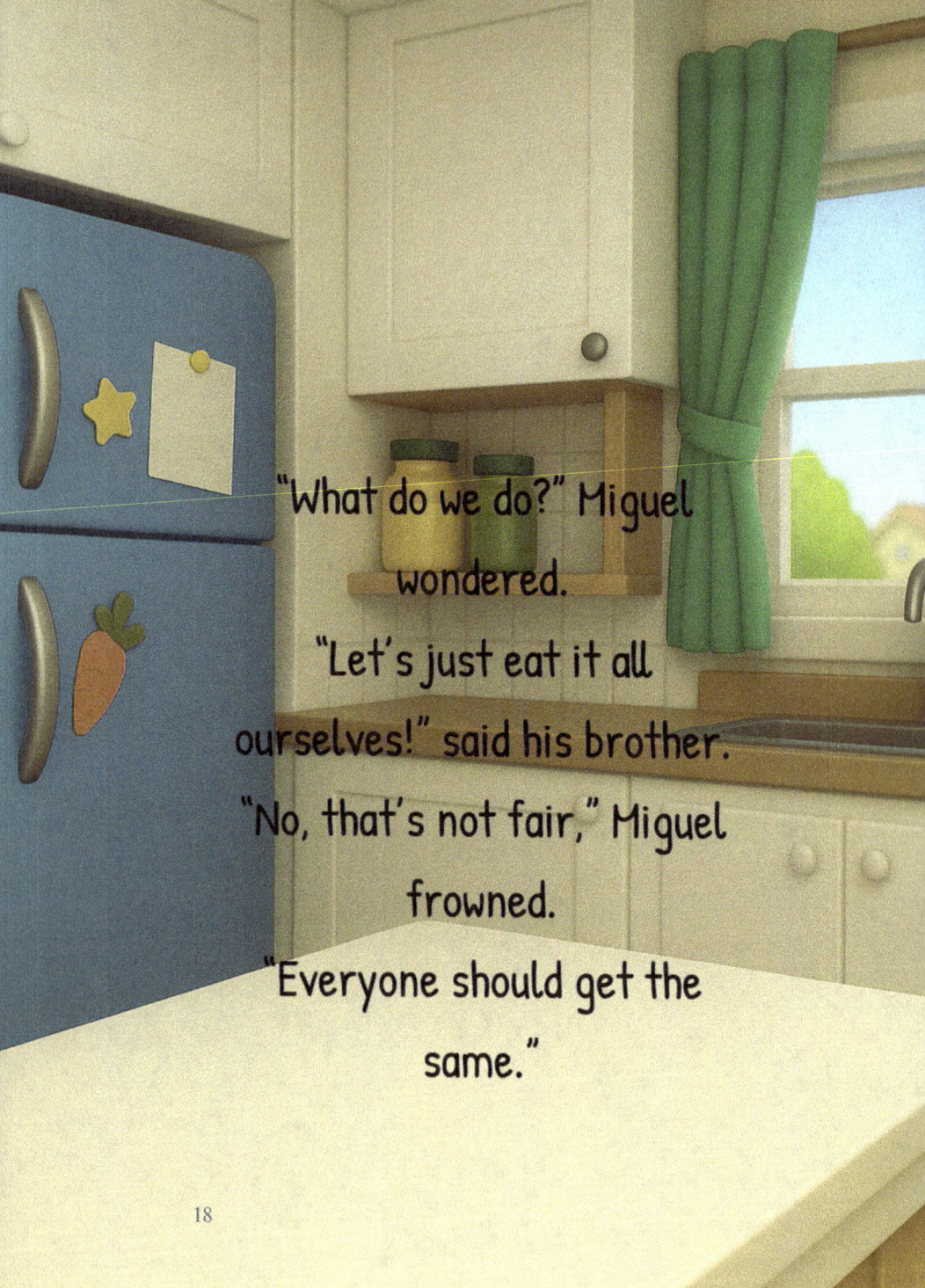

"What do we do?" Miguel wondered.

"Let's just eat it all ourselves!" said his brother.

"No, that's not fair," Miguel frowned. "Everyone should get the same."

The little brother grabbed a slice—
Miguel tried to stop him—
Splat!
The cake fell to the floor
And their puppy Toby
gobbled it up!

"Now, only three pieces are left!" The boys argued loudly— Until Mom and Dad came running into the kitchen.

"Time for a break," Mom said kindly.
"Let's eat breakfast and talk this out."
The family sat, ate, and listened.

"I just wanted it to be fair," Miguel said.
"We forgot Grandma and Grandpa," Dad nodded.
"We'll give them our slices," Mom smiled.

Miguel thought, then beamed:
"Let's bake a new cake and visit them!"
That way—everyone gets a piece.

And from that day on,
Miguel still loved fairness—
But he learned something
more important:
There's always a way to
share with love.